PRED

Terrorism

CONOR GEARTY

PHŒNIX

A PHOENIX PAPERBACK

First published in Great Britain in 1997 by
Phoenix, a division of the Orion Publishing Group Ltd
Orion House
5 Upper Saint Martin's Lane
London, WC2H 9EA

A CIP catalogue record for this book is available
from the British Library.

ISBN 0 297 81903 8

Typeset by SetSystems Ltd, Saffron Walden
Set in 9/13.5 Stone Serif
Printed in Great Britain by
Clays Ltd, St Ives plc

Contents

Introduction

In the final third of a twentieth century full of moral extremes, a new and virulent evil seems suddenly to be stalking the world, causing terrible violence without a thought and threatening the habit of democratic government wherever it has managed to throw down roots. This supposed enemy of freedom and liberty is not the fascist or communist ideologue of earlier eras against whom wars – both hot and cold – were waged for over seventy years. It is neither as powerful nor so explicit in its ambitions as either of its marauding predecessors, though this obscurity and anonymity are said merely to add to its strength. So powerful has its spell become that its name now describes our times. In the last decades of the twentieth century, it is said that we have been living in the 'age of terrorism'.

Seeming to have sprung suddenly upon us in 1968, the bloody imprints of this violent epoch are said now to be more evident and unmanageable than ever, in the return to violence in Northern Ireland and the Middle East and in the resurgence of such classical acts of terrorism as the 1996 hostage-taking at the Japanese ambassador's Peruvian residence. The violence is also frequently said to have taken on new and even more dangerous forms, such as with the release of poisonous gases in Tokyo's subway in 1995 and the forced ditching of a hijacked Ethiopian airliner in the Indian ocean in November 1996. Outbreaks of 'terrorism' are regularly presented in quasi-medical terms as symptoms of a contagious as well as an irrational phenomenon, providing no explanation for its actions as it spreads with alarming speed to previously secure locations. It is little wonder that in this supposed 'age of terrorism' anxious questions are increasingly being asked about the nature of Western society, about its apparent vulnerability to attacks of this 'terroristic' nature, and about the degree to which society's exposure to this new enemy now threatens its very survival. Terrorism seems like a modern bubonic plague, carried across borders by human rats and dedicated only to our arbitrary destruction.

It is very easy to get caught up in this transnational panic, particularly when its pessimistic version of reality is endlessly recycled by government ministers, the vast majority of the media and an apparently limitless stream of academic 'experts'. Every bloody incident by every dissident political group anywhere in the world, particularly if it involves Westerners, is instantaneously transformed into further evidence of this new wave of terror, regardless of any local factors or of any historical context that might more particularly explain it. The description of certain violence as 'terrorist' is now something that we take so much for granted that the word has rooted itself in our psyche, bringing with it all those intense anxieties about sudden and arbitrary violence with which as a society we have become preoccupied. So embedded have these assumptions now become that to question them openly, to ask whether there is any such thing as terrorism, or whether we are really in the midst of an 'age of terrorism', no longer provokes the bother of refutation so much as a look of sheer incomprehension. The 'age of terrorism' has become so blindingly obvious to all that the only public debate about the subject that now takes place concerns itself not with whether this worldwide disease actually exists but rather with how repressive and brutal we should be in trying to defeat it.

In light of this pervasive unanimity, the argument that follows might at first sight seem difficult to grasp, even a trifle eccentric. Any thinking which lies outside the mutually reinforcing world of the mainstream inevitably invites such labelling. Let us metaphorically nail four basic propositions to this introductory chapter, the literary equivalent of our front door, so that their oddity may be savoured before our defence of them begins. First, there is no 'age of terrorism'. Secondly, the concept of terrorism has never been a useful or intelligent way of describing political violence and the term is itself now more or less entirely meaningless. Thirdly, and only apparently para-doxically, terrorism as a subject has thrived precisely as a result of this intellectual vacuity, which governments have long recognized and cleverly exploited for their own ends. Fourthly, while democracy may indeed be threatened in this so-called 'age of terrorism', the danger to its integrity comes more from the terrorists' opponents, the states and their armed and police forces, than from the so-called terrorists themselves.

Let us now defend each of these heresies in turn and build our case for the expulsion from public affairs of this fruitless and tendentious preoccupation with a danger-ously meaningless label. If we do not act in this way, we face a future in which our political leaders might well succeed in panicking us into regarding our civil liberties as dangerous and therefore dispensable luxuries.

Chapter 1
History of a Modern Myth

We begin with this notion of an 'age of terrorism'. It suggests an era exclusively committed to a form of violence hitherto unknown to the world. In fact killing for political gain is as old as civil society itself, and causing terror to make a political point enjoys a similarly ancient if not always respectable pedigree. If this is what an 'age of terrorism' amounts to, then we have never been out of one. In the first century after the birth of Christ, Jewish radicals fought to free Palestine of Roman rule. According to Josephus, the Sicarii were 'brigands who took their name from a dagger carried in their bosom'. Their 'favourite trick' was 'to mingle with festival crowds, concealing under their garments small daggers with which they stabbed their opponents. When their victims fell the assassins melted into the indignant crowd, and through their plausibility entirely defied detection.' The Assassins a millennium later emerged from the same troublesome part of the world and anticipated in the reactions that they stimulated many of the anxieties that dog our 'age of terrorism'. They belonged to the Ismaeli sect of the Shia branch of the Islamic faith and were active in the twelfth and thirteenth centuries. Their contemporary notoriety in the West lay in their preparedness to assassinate the leaders of the Crusades that were then ravaging the Holy Land, with Conrad of Montferrat being their most famous victim, killed in 1192.

The Sicarii and the Assassins would fit easily into most

contemporary definitions of terrorism, and they inspired the same degree of fear and loathing among their respective political establishments as our own brand of 'terrorists' do today. The events that actually gave birth to the word in its modern sense, however, involved terror orchestrated not by rebels acting in defiance of governmental authority but by the forces of a state itself. The Oxford English Dictionary first mentions the word in 1795, after the post-revolutionary Terror in France had accounted for the death of thousands in a short period of deliberate horror between 1792 and 1794. It was precisely because the state was involved that it proved so easy to kill so many. Not for the first time, and certainly not for the last, the power of a government to kill was shown to be far greater than that of any merely rebellious group, harassed as such subversives invariably are by the forces of a hostile state and forced to operate as they must always do without the benefit of a state team of authorized killers, willing to execute their every wish. When the stimulus of the French Revolution had precipitated a largely ineffectual insurgency in Ireland, the revenge killings on which the British government then embarked exceeded in their number the total of casualties for the whole period of the French Terror. Here again was a glimpse into the future, the 'counter-terrorism' of the authorities causing infinitely more 'terror' than the mischief at which it was purportedly aimed.

It has been a grievous mistake to lose sight of this first meaning of terrorism as 'government by intimidation as directed and carried out by the party in power'. In this neglect lies the origin of the current belief that our age is unprecedentedly swamped with terrorist violence. Somewhere along the line after the French Revolution and before the First World War, 'terrorism' ceased to connote what the word primarily seems to suggest, the bloody but straightforward business of causing terror to achieve political ends, in other words a tactic of violent action available to and capable of being deployed by any actor in a conflict situation, whether it be war, civil war or popular revolution, and whether the actor be a warring state, the government itself or a faction of the governed. In place of this simple approach, emphasizing the 'terror' in terrorism, the meaning of the word gradually changed during the nineteenth century in three vital ways. First, terrorism grew to be identified exclusively with subversive violence. Secondly, it came to be applied to such violence, even in situations in which it did not involve terrorizing the ordinary population. Thirdly, and flowing from both of these, terrorism came to represent a self-standing method of violent subversion which was different in kind from other types of conflict. The result of this linguistic upheaval was that, by the start of the twentieth century, 'terrorism' no longer described the tactic of causing terror, capable of being deployed by anyone in a conflict, but meant something quite technical instead, the use of violence by political subversives who were engaged in such methods in isolation and not as part of a wider conflict. This meant that states and armies engaged in conventional or civil war could not properly be described as 'terrorist' even when they were engaged in terrorizing either their own citizens or the people of an opposing force.

We have been paying a price for these attenuations of meaning ever since they first crept into the language. This is not the fault of the era which produced them. In the relatively tranquil nineteenth century, the fashion for political assassination produced a generation of optimistic tyrannicides, whose enjoyment of the 'terrorist' label helped to shape its meaning, even though the terror they were causing, if they were causing any at all, was to a tiny and extremely well-guarded élite. Terrorism, wrote one whose group had made a series of attempts on the life of Tsar Alexander II, 'directs its blows against the real perpetrators of evil'. Another Russian, writing in 1883, wrote of the terrorist that he was 'noble, terrible, irresistibly fascinating, for he combine[d] in himself the two sublimities of human grandeur: the martyr and the hero'. Of course there was also political violence in Europe which caused terror to innocent civilians as well, such as that in which the Irish Fenians were involved with their dynamite campaigns in Britain in 1883–4 and 1903–5, but the fact that this violence was frequently subversive rather than state-sponsored tended further to confirm the movement of the idea of terrorism away from its late-eighteenth-century French origins.

The concept of terrorism suggested by these nineteenth-century precedents meant that it occurred to no one to describe the horrors of the Western and Russian fronts in the First World War as acts of terrorism. In the 1930s, however, it was as 'terrorism' that the problem of a series of political assassinations was expressed. After the King of Yugoslavia and the Foreign Minister of France were killed by Croatian nationalists in Marseilles in 1934, the League of Nations felt compelled to become involved, setting up a committee of experts to study the problem. In due course two international conventions appeared, on such apparently contemporary concerns as the prevention and punishment of terrorism and the establishment of an international criminal court. Though both conventions were adopted in 1937, neither came into force. It is salutary to consider why this should have been so. By the end of the 1930s, the international community had lost its zeal for feeling anxious about the terrorism which had earlier given rise to such concern. The energy that had generated the intervention by the League of Nations could neither be sustained nor mustered afresh.

Though the problem of terrorism in the sense of political assassinations was no longer a great concern, this did not mean that the issue of violent subversion, or the still larger question of political terror – or terrorism in its original pre-nineteenth-century sense – had also ceased any longer to matter. If anything the reverse had occurred. The use of terror for political ends increased enormously in scale, extending far beyond the focused assassinations of earlier years, at just the moment that 'terrorism' as such was drifting off the international agenda. Indeed, and even more peculiarly, it was precisely because of this huge increase in terror that 'terrorism' as a discrete problem lost its force. What happened was that with the onset of the Second World War and for its duration between 1939 and 1945, political terror became just one means among many through which a great global conflagration was fought. Whereas, in the peaceful inter-war era and before that in the nineteenth century, terrorism had been frequently to the forefront of public concern because it had been one of only a very few forms of political subversion that was then manifesting itself in violence, during the world war that followed its subversive activities were quickly swamped by the depth and range of military operations that surrounded it. The paradoxical consequence of this is that the age of greatest political terror this century is never thought of as an 'age of terrorism', whereas the relatively peaceful times either side of that war have been frequently so described.

We can see this very clearly by considering the effect of

an IRA bombing campaign in Britain which began in January 1939 with an ultimatum to the British government to withdraw from Northern Ireland. Here was a terrorist campaign in both the narrow and the broad meaning of the word, in that not only was a violent, subversive group involved but also the methods that were used caused indiscriminate injury to civilians. In the months that followed the IRA's declaration of intent, a series of explosions caused a number of injuries and fatalities, culminating in an horrific bomb which exploded in Coventry's main shopping area on 25 August 1939, killing five people and injuring more than fifty. Perhaps in less peculiar times this campaign would have engendered a climate of fear and anxiety about terrorism similar to that which was to grip Great Britain in 1972–4 and which had briefly threatened to dominate Victorian public life in 1883. Certainly the terrorism seemed more severe than that which had caused such an international rumpus just a few short years before. But, with war with Germany breaking out on 3 September 1939, there was not enough space in the public imagination for the kind of panic that such arbitrary killings would normally have provoked. Nor was a busy government inclined to foster public fear. After one legislative response and some quietly effective police action, the campaign ground unnoticed to a halt in 1940. Its attacks on civilians, though dreadful, were lost in the nightmare of a truly catastrophic war, one which claimed the lives of 30,000 civilians through bombing attacks in Britain alone in its first twenty months. During one night in Coventry in November 1940, German bombers killed more than one hundred times the number of people the IRA had blown up in their attack in the same town the year before.

Our intuitive reluctance to class the many acts of terror associated with the military conduct of the Second World War as 'terrorist' shows how far the word has drifted from its roots. If we take the idea of political terror at face value, as encompassing at its core the arbitrary killing of civilians for political purposes in a way which terrifies the populace, then it is beyond dispute that the war involved both subversive terror and state terror on a truly dramatic scale. We need only think of the French Resistance and Tito's partisans for evidence of the first, and mention the names of Coventry, Dresden and Hiroshima for proof of the second. Some of us might want to argue in the context of the Second World War that attacks on the established pro-Nazi regimes in France or Yugoslavia were justified at the time, just as many of us would remember with admiration the bravery of those German officers who sought at great risk to themselves to assassinate Hitler during the latter part of the war. In the same vein, there is still a lively debate about whether it was right or wrong to use the atomic bomb in Japan in 1945, though nobody (even those who have profoundly disagreed with the decision) has called President Truman a 'state terrorist' for having ordered it.

We are all shy of using the language of terrorism in this way in wartime, despite the fact that such conduct invariably involved the indiscriminate killing of civilians for political ends or to communicate a political message, all supposedly classic ingredients of pure acts of terror. Our reluctance on this score is understandable, and is derived from more than a technical appreciation of the artificial and academic distinction between 'terror' and 'terrorism' that crept into the language in the nineteenth century. It is rooted in a legitimate anxiety about the moral baggage that the word 'terrorism' now carries with it. Intuitively we see the question of the possible morality of many of these wartime acts of terror and violent subversion as not being beyond argument. It might have been right or it might have been wrong to kill this or that Vichy official, to order attacks on German cities to undermine the morale of the ordinary German people, or even to kill millions of Japanese so as to force an end to the war. The point about deployment of the language of terrorism is that the mere use of the word implies that that judgement has already been made. To call an act of violence a terrorist act is not so much to describe it as to condemn it, subjugating all questions of context and circumstance to the reality of its immorality.

These various points can be reinforced by considering the violence that accompanied the campaigns for freedom from colonial rule that were such a marked feature of the post-war world. In the twenty or so years after the defeat of Germany and Japan, an array of peoples across the globe wrenched themselves free from European domination. This series of transitions to independence was frequently accompanied by political violence. In Malaya, Kenya, Cyprus and Aden, British authorities gave in only unwillingly to a pressure for liberation in which calculated, political killing played an important part. The French immersed their nation in even deeper strife, fighting themselves to a standstill in Indochina in the early 1950s and then engaging with Algerian nationalism in a bloody eight-year feud, culminating in the conceding of independence to the country in 1962. These wars of liberation were conducted by subversive forces prepared to fight for their cause in any way that was available to them, whether it be constitutional or illegal. Such tactics frequently included engaging the colonial establishment in the countryside as rural guerrillas and in the cities as covert bombers. They faced states prepared on occasion (as in Algeria) to engage in massive retaliatory terror so as to avert or at least to delay defeat.

Despite the seriousness, depth and bloodiness of these various conflicts, their combined impact was not such as to cause their times to be described as constituting an 'age of terrorism'. This was not because there were no assaults on civilians. The battle for Algiers in 1956–7 involved a campaign of bombing in the city, and many of the other conflicts such as in Aden and Kenya included similarly indiscriminate attacks on civilians. Just as with the Second World War, however, it was the wide-ranging nature of these hostilities that made the terrorist label inappropriate. The situations they encompassed were too serious to be accurately described by such a label. A deeper inhibition on the successful use of the 'terrorist' epithet also existed, rooted in Europe's equivocation about the morality of these wars of independence. Close to the surface in each colonial state lay a body of opinion sympathetic to the aims, if not necessarily the actual violence, of its opponents. Local rebels typically enjoyed wide popular support for both. This popular following underpinned not only rural but also urban military activity of a frequency and force of which contemporary European groups in today's 'age of terrorism' would not be remotely capable. To many among the colonizers as well as the colonized, the struggle for independence was a noble ideal which if it did not justify might at least excuse the means that the fighters deemed essential to its realization. In such a complex environment, the simplistic language of 'terrorism', with its inherent moral condemnation of all subversive violence, was neither appropriate nor frequently successfully deployed. We do not call this colonial phase an 'age of terrorism', because it involved more serious violence than we normally associate with terrorism and also because, just as was the case with the Second World War, we want to reserve our right not to condemn all of the violence that then occurred.

What then are we to make of this 'age of terrorism' in which the experts tell us we have been immersed since 1968? Viewed in historical context, it is clear that the decades since this supposed turning point have for the West at least been a time of unusual peace and stability. There have been a few wars, but these have stayed well clear of the West's public thoroughfares. The colonial insurgencies that had involved the European powers in so much post-war political violence had more or less wound down by 1968, with those that remained (such as in South Africa and Rhodesia) being now mainly squabbles between indigenous peoples and the colonial settlers rather than between the natives and the states who had once sent those settlers there. There had been terrorist campaigns in Europe during the age of decolonization, such as in Northern Ireland between 1956 and 1962 and in South Tyrol during the same period, but, just as was the case with the IRA during the Second World War, these fairly innocuous outbreaks of violence had made little impact. It has been the atmosphere of confident tranquillity that we have enjoyed since 1968 that has allowed the kind of political killing that we have come to describe as terrorism to grab the public imagination in a way that has been out of all proportion to the harm that such acts have achieved. As we have seen, it is of the essence of such violence as it has come to be understood that it takes place in isolation, unconnected to any greater conflict, and that it is subversive in nature. This has been the only sort of political violence on which the West has been at the receiving end for more than three decades. There has therefore been space in the public mind for an emotional reaction, for the sort of neurotic anxiety that would not have been induced had such violence been no more than an unnoticed sideshow in a Western world of greater bloodshed.

Without any great war or massive insurgency to distract us, we have been able to indulge our anxieties about the terrorists' sporadic violence. Concern about 'terrorism' in the West is therefore paradoxically reassuring, since contriving the level of passion that we have voiced about such a minor problem could only be possible in a time of relative peace. The point can be reinforced by considering exactly how much of this political violence there has been during this 'age of terrorism'. The evidence is complicated by difficulties of definition, but whatever yardstick is chosen the numbers of casualties remain historically extremely low. If we restrict ourselves to political violence which crosses borders or is otherwise international in character, the figure for the number of fatalities since the 1960s is on any statistical basis in the low thousands. Certainly there has been no year in which any agency, think-tank or research group, no matter how enthusiastically or expansively it has defined its subject, has ever managed to find more than a thousand fatalities a year from 'international terrorism'. If we add in domestic terrorism, but hold to the notion of such violence being essentially subversive in nature and separate from other types of military conflict, we still arrive at a figure which is in the tens of thousands at the very most.

Dreadful though each of these casualties has been for

the victims and families concerned, these figures surely cry out to be seen in proportion. Not only are they historically extremely low, but they also represent only a tiny fraction of the deaths from political violence that have occurred across the world since the supposed outbreak of terrorism in 1968. This is where the self-centredness of the West's habit of treating terrorism as a special isolated type of violence capable of being engaged in only by subversives is at its most exposed. There is an unattractive irony in the fact that during this 'age of terrorism' the number of deaths from what is counted in these statistics as 'terrorism' has been dwarfed by the casualties from the civil wars, communal disorders, genocidal attacks and other forms of political terror that have been gathering pace across the world. The state-orchestrated terrorism of certain homicidal Central American governments in the 1980s alone caused more deaths than the whole catalogue of subversive, terrorist violence since 1968. The victims of political terror in Rwanda, the former Yugoslavia and Somalia in the 1990s have not been included in any statistics on 'terrorism'. The problem of 'terrorism' as it is commonly understood in Europe and North America is very much a Western construct. Its victims may be few but the subject is so defined and its parameters are so arranged that they are almost exclusively Western. In this time of political peace for the West, terrorism represents one of the very few ways in which a European or American can die as a result of political violence. Talk of an 'age of terrorism' shows merely that the West is not content only to control our world, it wants also to define our times.

Chapter 2
Seeds of Confusion

The notion of an 'age of terrorism' is so ahistorical and counter-factual that its grip on the public imagination cannot be wholly explained simply by pointing to the lack of other forms of political terror competing for the attention of the Western mind. There are lots of (non-political) ways of dying in the West which are both as terrifying as terrorism and at the same time far more frequent, but which despite their prevalence attract not a fraction of the levels of anxiety which terrorism seems to provoke. This is an obvious point and it might also seem at first glance a mystifying one. The idea of terrorism has not however made it to the top of the international agenda solely through its own efforts. The casualty list has not been the only engine powering its rise to dismal notoriety. The whole concept of a terrorist plague has secured a convenient ally in the form of the many powerful authorities around the world who find themselves immersed in domestic challenges to their own political supremacy. Whereas the concept of terrorism in its modern form may have been Western in origin, this has not stopped states from other parts of the world adopting its language of condemnation. Indeed, for all such governments, whether Western or not, the notion of a wave of terrorism afflicting the entire globe is a tempting and consoling way of characterizing their own problems. It allows them to divert attention away from the local context of such insubordination, which can at times be revealingly embarrassing for the states concerned. In place of this domestic focus, the language of terrorism offers an attractive new emphasis on the international nature of a state's plight, with all nations now seemingly yoked together in courageous adversity like some recently formed brotherhood of victims. It is this neat diversionary trick, not the statistics on subversive violence, which has largely fuelled the terrorist panic that has supposedly gripped the world since 1968.

This can be more clearly seen by considering the uncertainty that continues to surround the meaning of terrorism. Of course the idea of terrorism as inherently subversive in nature, as something that only rebels do, is now deeply embedded in the language, to the advantage of established orders everywhere. Within this restrictive parameter, however, the way governments and national legal systems view the term has drifted apart from the public perception of what constitutes terrorism. That there is any difference between the two may come as something of a surprise. The least you would expect after decades in the international spotlight and endless academic studies would be a fairly clear indication of what terrorism means, making it possible quickly to label this or that act across the world as falling within or without some agreed definition. In fact no such agreement exists. There can be few subjects which are so loud in their claims while being simultaneously so devoid of coherence. One particularly determined scholar once combed through 109 different definitions and produced a set of no fewer than twenty-two components that are to be found in the academic literature from time to time. He did expose a few elements that appeared more frequently than others and which most people would probably intuitively feel to be part and parcel of the quintessential terrorist act. The classic terrorist act in this sense would involve a random attack by subversives on innocent individuals, intended to cause fear, death and injury and thereby to secure political concessions from somebody or some organization other than those who were being directly attacked. This certainly captures the aircraft hijack, the hostage seizure and the arbitrary no-warning bomb, all of which immediately and explicably attract the 'terrorist' label. These were the sorts of incidents that first sparked off speculation about a new 'terrorist age' in the West in the late 1960s.

The subversive violence that became apparent at this time came from three sources in particular. There can be no doubt that the pseudo-colonial violence of groups like ETA and the IRA, the ideological subversion of the likes of the Red Brigades and the RAF and the Palestinian-inspired violence of this period bore many of these hallmarks of classic terrorism. It is this sort of violence that the public generally still has in mind when the image of the terrorist and of the terrorist act is brought to its attention. The idea of terror, of the arbitrary attack on the innocent, remains firmly at the forefront of the word. To governments, however, the word terrorism has come to connote something far broader than this, and broader even than the targeted assassinations of earlier eras. It is now officially construed in terms which are wide enough to encompass within their condemnatory remit all subversive violence of every sort. The popular perception of terrorism as indiscriminate terror has been fanning the judgemental fire inherent in the word, but it has been the official, wider meaning of the word that has driven the counter-terrorist energies of the state, not only in the West where as we have seen concern about terrorism originated, but throughout the rest of the world as well, with many nations wanting for their own opportunistic reasons to climb aboard this anti-terrorist bandwagon. It is this disparity of meaning between the popular and official meanings of terrorism that has made the subject both incomprehensible and at the same time vulnerable to exploitation by governments, both internally and as part of their international diplomacy. This latter manipulation, which we shall consider in our next chapter, has only been possible because of weaknesses that have been present from the start in the whole concept of terrorism. For even when the term was being deployed in its most credible and coherent of manners, as was the case during this brief period at the end of the 1960s and the start of the 1970s, it was nevertheless even then a confusing and distracting label to attach to the conflicts that it sought to describe. It has been the festering of problems ignored or glossed over then that has been instrumental in precipitating the dangerous chaos that has now engulfed the whole subject and which threatens our future freedom.

Let us now develop this point by looking more closely at the problems that gave rise to our so-called 'age of terrorism'. If we turn first to the upsurge of pseudo-colonial subversion, it is clear that the violence that had become a familiar part of the ritual of decolonization in the 1950s and 1960s took an unexpected turn in about 1968. In Spain in that year, the ETA movement which had been established in 1959 claimed the chief of the political police in the Guipúzcoa province as its first victim in its renewed struggle for Basque freedom. A year later, the always potentially unstable political situation in Northern Ireland exploded into the public eye, with the previously moribund IRA gaining a new lease of life from the disorder that suddenly engulfed the Province. In October 1970, members of the FLQ (the Quebec Liberation Front) kidnapped the British trade commissioner James Cross and Pierre Laporte, a minister in the provincial government of Quebec, killing the latter after an attempted escape. All of these movements were quickly deplored by their respective governments as terrorist, and their violence fitted at least one meaning of this term to the extent that it was both subversive and isolated from other forms of insurgency. Unlike the putative assassins of the nineteenth century, however, these groups eschewed entirely the terrorist label and looked instead to the recent tradition of anti-colonial militancy for inspiration and moral legitimacy. This was not as irrational as their opponents might have wanted to believe.

The success of the post-war guerilla campaigns that had produced so many new independent nations had had the effect of making the now expanded international community more inclined than it might previously have been to accept the right of a people to wage a war of liberation against its political masters. This became more apparent than ever just as these violent nationalist campaigns were getting under way. In 1970, the United Nations General Assembly gave its overwhelming support to a Declaration of Principles of International Law Concerning Friendly Relations and Co-operation among States which proclaimed the right of a people to self-determination and to seek outside help for such a struggle. This was followed in 1974 by a further UN initiative which accepted that the concept of international armed conflict should be expanded to include 'armed conflicts in which peoples are fighting against colonial domination and alien occupation and against racist regimes in the exercise of their right of self-determination . . .'. This formulation was added to the Geneva Conventions in 1977, and its effect was inevitably to add further legitimacy to the notion of a liberation struggle by a guerrilla army. All of this international movement was primarily aimed at justifying the battles of the past and at legitimizing the liberation struggles that were still taking place in Africa, against white rule in South Africa and Rhodesia and against the continuing Portuguese presence in other parts of the continent. One of its effects, however, was to appear to underpin other secessionist struggles outside the colonial mainstream, not least within apparently homogeneous national entities in the developed world.

Supporters of the ETA movement in Spain and the IRA in Northern Ireland saw their respective political situations in essentially colonial terms, with both organizations doing no more than exercising their right to struggle on behalf of their respective peoples for their liberation from colonial domination. From the start the analogy was more apparent than real. Spain and the United Kingdom regarded these provinces not as alien colonial outposts but as integral parts of their respective nations, with the secession of either of them being akin more to the amputation of a limb than to the jettisoning of an unwanted appendage. Reflecting this sense of unity, the population in both areas was by no means exclusively drawn from the culture on whose behalf independence was being claimed. In the four Basque provinces in Spain, approximately 65 per cent of the population were native Basques. In Northern Ireland the Irish nationalist community was even lower, amounting to not much more than 40 per cent of the population. Inevitably given these demographic facts, there was no support for the kind of broad fronts that had earlier provided vital support for the push for freedom in genuinely colonial situations. Not even the bulk of the nationalistically inclined communities in either place viewed subversive violence as a regrettable but necessary means to a desired end, as had whole swathes of opinion in such places as Aden and Algeria.

In these circumstances it was inevitable that neither ETA nor the IRA should ever have been strong enough to mount a guerrilla campaign from secured territory or to reach across the whole community so as to make their homelands ungovernable from the notionally hated centre. Isolated subversive violence was all that there was left to do, a consolation for aspiring guerrillas too feeble to mount a proper struggle. It is in this sense that it is correct to describe terrorism as the 'weapon of the weak'. Initially both movements tried to keep the guerrilla model to the forefront of their minds by targeting only specific and (in their view) clearly culpable representatives of the 'oppressive' regime, or by engaging only in actions designed to popularize themselves among their local communities. They tried in other words to keep well outside the popular understanding of the terrorist as the purveyor of indiscriminate terror while recognizing that it was inevitable that they would be so described by their antagonistic governments. We have already seen that ETA's first victim was a local chief of police. In January 1972, the movement kidnapped an industrialist, releasing him only after his company had agreed to rehire 120 dismissed employees, increase the wages of the workforce and grant a measure of worker participation in the management of the company. Another short kidnap a year later produced a similarly attractive package for local workers. In December 1973 ETA managed to assassinate the Prime Minister Admiral Luis Carrero Blanco in a daring attack reminiscent of the tyrannicide preached by nineteenth-century terrorists. For its part, the IRA's violence was initially almost wholly defensive in nature, acting on behalf of its community against both communal and state aggression. When it went on the offensive, its first actions were against police officers and soldiers on duty and other explicit upholders of the allegedly alien British presence.

Existentially pleasing though all this busy and sometimes dramatic violence might have been to both ETA and the IRA, and more militaristic than terrorist though it may have appeared to their respective local communities, it was not obviously leading anywhere. The problem with isolated subversive violence directed at the forces of the state is firstly that it rarely has a sufficient impact to compel any response other than the obvious one of greater repression and secondly that it becomes much harder to pull off after the first few coups, when the forces of the state have inevitably regrouped and improved their defences against sudden urban attack. This had been the clear lesson of the urban guerrilla movements in South America in the 1960s, which had begun full of noble intentions, only to end in a welter of state counter-terror and increasingly indiscriminate subversive violence. This is exactly what happened in both Spain and Ireland during the 1970s and 1980s. As the years proceeded, more and more of the victims of ETA and the IRA came to have less and less connection with the regimes which both movements claimed to be attacking. The notion of the legitimate target was expanded so as to include the vulnerable and exposed as well as the security forces and government ministers, now largely speaking fully insulated from attack. In three years at the end of the 1970s, no fewer than 220 people died in ETA-related violence, many of them unconnected with any supposedly culpable target. As early as 1972 the IRA were blowing up restaurants, hotels and bars and in 1974 a series of attacks in Britain culminated in the blowing up of two public houses in Birmingham, resulting in twenty-one dead and 162 injured, many of the latter horribly maimed. The launching of deliberately or at least recklessly indiscriminate attacks has been a feature of both conflicts in Northern Ireland and Spain ever since.

There can be little doubt therefore that both ETA and the IRA quite quickly reached the point where much of their subversive violence could properly be described as entailing acts of political terror, in the core sense of involving indiscriminate attacks against civilians, designed to inspire fear and thereby to communicate a political message to a wider audience. They had become 'terrorists' in both the popular and the governmental meanings of the word. Despite this, it is by no means clear that affixing this 'terrorist' label to either organization has been at all helpful to understanding or resolving either of the two problems of which they are the most obvious manifestations. The value-laden connotations of the phrase, with its assumption that any activity described as terrorist is necessarily morally wrong, inevitably skews the proper understanding of a difficult and complex situation. Whether it is used loosely to mean all subversive violence or more tightly to describe subversive acts of pure terror, the language of terrorism is the enemy of context, forcing the analysis of any situation down a blind alley of anger at certain violence and blindness towards the rest. It blinkers the discussion of any particular political problem which has manifested itself in violence by compelling a concentration on that violence to the exclusion of the broader picture. From the subversive group's point of view, the definition of terrorism seems contrived so as to produce only one result: moral condemnation of its violence to the exclusion of all larger questions.

The 'terrorist expert' will thus rarely feel obliged to observe that the Spain in which ETA grew to maturity was a fascist state with such habits of repression that the leaders of the relatively quiescent Basque Nationalist Party (PNV) had had to seek the safety of exile in France. The PNV had been in government in the region when Guernica had been destroyed during the Civil War, an act of terror far more barbaric than the worst of ETA excesses, but rarely classed as such in the catalogues of terrorism, on account merely of its having been part of a wider conflict. Admiral Blanco was the last great devotee of fascism and Franco's heir apparent when ETA's brutal removal of him from the political scene made far easier the transition to democracy that subsequently occurred. These are vital facts in any assessment of the legitimacy of ETA's subversive campaign, just as are those that demonstrate how democratic Spain has transformed the basis of the group's claim to freedom. Also important, but obscured by the restriction of the label of terrorism to subversive groups, is the extent to which the tactic of political terror has not been exclusively the preserve of ETA. The hysterically repressive reaction of Franco's Spain to the first ETA killing in 1968 caused more terror to more people than ETA had managed in its first decade of existence. Even democratic Spain has been forced to confront serious allegations of death squads operating against ETA's political associates on behalf of the government. The problem with the 'terrorist' label is not just that we assume all terrorism to be bad; it is also that we naturally consider the reverse also to be true, that everything called 'counter-terrorism' must be good. Such naïvety is a temptation even to democratic governments.

Very similar points can be made in relation to Northern Ireland, about the inequality, discrimination and partisan law enforcement in the Province which had oppressed the nationalist community since the partition of Ireland in 1922, and about the alleged torture, the killings on Bloody Sunday in January 1972 and the other state reactions that followed upon the outbreak of disorder. The point is not at all necessarily to justify any of this subversive violence solely by having regard to its context. It is more modestly to assert that there is such a context, that this violence – some of it certainly horrific, but some of it also undoubtedly highly focused and quasi-military in its execution – comes not from some homeless world plague of terrorism but rather from highly particular parts of the world, with long histories, deep traditions and a series of specific and complicated relations. The simplicity of the terrorist label may be seductive and at times understandable but the effect of the acontextual moralizing inherent in the phrase is to divert public discussion down an intellectual cul-de-sac, thereby invariably prolonging the conflict it is desired to resolve, since it is only by addressing political causes that subversive violence can be properly confronted.

We can also see the same process at work with the second form of subversive violence that burst upon the international scene in the late 1960s as part of this supposed new wave of terrorism. The most prominent of this category of ideological subversives who took their dissent into the realm of the criminal were the Baader–Meinhof group in Germany (afterwards known as the Red Army Faction), the Red Brigades in Italy and the United Red Army in Japan. All three have followed the grim path to ever more arbitrary violence that has invariably characterized the practitioners of isolated political violence of this sort. Without cultural roots as deep as those enjoyed by ETA and the IRA, none of these groups has achieved as much destruction or has endured as effectively as either of these organizations. Nevertheless their driving force has in many ways been an updated version of what had once driven the earlier generation of anti-colonials – a fierce anger against imperialism in general and US imperialism in particular. These groups saw that it was possible to control a country without going to the bother of governing it. This was the excess of which the United States stood accused in the three countries in which these groups operated, West Germany, Italy and Japan. The early impetus for their subversion came from the United States' engagement in Vietnam. Many of their targets were American, and their leaders frequently sought to explain their actions by adverting to what was going on in South-east Asia. There was certainly something odd about the huge concentration on Baader–Meinhof and Red Brigades violence in Europe, of which there was very little, at a time when the US was engaged in a variety of types of horrific political terror as part of its war effort in Vietnam. This violence was however not 'terrorist' because it enjoyed the full force of a state behind it and was not isolated in its execution. So specialized has our definition of terrorism become that, just as was the case during the Second World War, it would seem that the more terrible the act of political terror, and the greater the violence that accompanies it, the less likely it is that it will be classed as terrorism.

All these points come together in the Middle East, which provided the third great platform for the leap into the 'age of terrorism' that supposedly occurred around 1968. It was Palestinian violence above all else that first engendered and then fuelled the panic about terrorism with which we are now so familiar. Viewed in isolation, there is little doubt that there was a sudden upsurge both in 'terrorism' and in 'international terrorism' in the region at this time, however either term is defined. In November 1968 a bomb exploded in a crowded marketplace in Jerusalem, killing twelve people (ten of whom were Jewish) and injuring fifty-five. The explosive was concealed in a parked car. Other bombs followed and in October 1969 five apartment buildings in Haifa were blown up, killing two Israelis and injuring twenty people. The Palestinian quarrel with Israel was also taken on to the world stage at this time, with an El Al jet being hijacked as early as July 1968, but with the pivotal moment of this sort coming in September 1970 when no fewer than 575 hostages were taken in the course of the hijacking of four jet airliners, all of which were dramatically destroyed after the release of the hostages had been successfully negotiated. In the years that followed, Palestinian violence continued to gather pace in the Middle East and at the same time took on a seedier, more desperate and brutal form on its trips abroad. In May 1972, an indiscriminate assault at Lod International Airport near Tel Aviv claimed twenty-eight civilian lives, among whom were sixteen Puerto Rican pilgrims on their way to visit Christian shrines in the Holy Land. In September 1972 came the famous assault on the Israeli quarters at the Munich Olympics, in which a total of seventeen people were killed.

All of this Palestinian violence was of course terrorism in its core sense of involving the terrorizing of innocent civilians in order to communicate a political message. Even when the terror was at its worst, however, the language of terrorism was hiding more than it revealed. The Israeli state whose leaders now reviled these actions as 'international terrorism' had itself been at least partly produced by similar conduct in the past, most notably the bombing of the King David Hotel in Jerusalem in 1946, in which ninety-one people died, fifty-four of them civilians. After the formation of the state, the application of political terror had been one of the prime means by which Israeli territory had been expanded and the control of its armed forces over the region consolidated. In the decades before 1968, the Palestinian deaths at the hands of Israeli forces at such villages as Qibya and Kafr Qasem were etched into the minds of the people in the way that the bombing of Guernica had imprinted itself on the Basques. None of any of this was 'terrorism' because it was all done by the forces of the state. The Arab nations did attempt to wage formal war in 1967 but it was a counter-productive disaster, leading to the loss to Israel of vast tracts of land that had earlier escaped invasion. In the aftermath of the Six Day War, the Palestinian Liberation Organization initially sought in true anti-colonial fashion to mount a proper guerrilla campaign against the Israeli presence in the Occupied Territories, but this floundered on the reality of a far superior military enemy which had not the slightest intention of throwing in the towel. Just as with ETA and the IRA, 'terrorism' seemed the only alternative to passive acquiescence. In their 'will', published in Damascus, the dead Palestinians who had been responsible for the Munich attack wrote of their desire for the world to 'know of the existence of a people whose country has been occupied for twenty-four years, and their honour trampled underfoot. . . . There is no harm if the youth of the world understand their tragedy for a few hours.' In the aerial strikes that Israel launched against Syria and Lebanon in the months after Munich, it was reported that hundreds of civilians were killed. That these were not within the Western definition of terrorism was no consolation to the victims, but it does explain why their deaths, like so many Palestinian losses before and since, went largely unnoticed and unreported.

Chapter 3
The Dangerous Utility of an Illusion

We may conclude from this brief survey that even in the darkest age of terrorism, between 1968 and 1974, when arbitrary political violence of a terrifying nature was at its height in the West, the use of the language of terrorism caused more problems than it resolved. The preoccupation with terrorism served only to replace the careful analysis of specific issues with wild, panic searches for general causes, and to divert attention away from real difficulties on to spurious issues, such as the tactics of terrorism or the psychology of the terrorist, as though the rebels under discussion were a type of genetic mutant. In the years that have followed this early phase, governments the world over have exploited the combination of intellectual vacuity and moral judgement inherent in the terrorist label in a way that has hugely facilitated the repressive powers of the states concerned while at the same time greatly confusing the search for solutions to many difficult international problems. The most grievous damage has been done in authoritarian states, already repressive by nature, for whom the Western language of 'terrorism' has been a propaganda godsend, allowing them to present their domestic opponents in a guise that is bound to be anathema to influential world (that is, Western) opinion, and then dealing with them brutally and invisibly, as terrorists rather than as the heroic freedom-fighters that they have all too frequently been.

The most extreme example of such linguistic freeloading

occurred in Central and South America during the 1970s and 1980s, where the supposed necessity for strong counter-terrorist action masked state terror of almost unbelievable brutality, by a variety of military regimes whose power was exercised without even a fig-leaf of democratic legitimacy. The 'urban guerrillas' in Brazil and Uruguay were brutally repressed by the mid-1970s, and during the 'dirty war' that followed shortly afterwards in Argentina it has been estimated that over 10,000 people 'disappeared'. In the 1980s, the deaths of civilians caused by Central American military juntas in the name of 'counter-terrorism' reached into the tens of thousands. The levels of terror achieved by these governments and the numbers of killings in which they were involved exceeded, out of all proportion, the subversive violence with which they were purportedly confronted. Throughout even the worst of these excesses the West's preoccupation with the need for strong action against terrorism inoculated its leaders to the political context in which these military rulers were operating.

A similar process occurred in South Africa. As early as 1967, the apartheid government had statutorily defined terrorism as any activity likely to 'endanger the maintenance of law and order'. Not content with such generalities, the legislation went on to specify as terrorist any conduct which promoted 'general dislocation, disturbance or disorder', 'prejudice' to 'any industry or undertaking' or 'embarrassment' to the 'administration of the affairs of the State'. This was not the end of it by any means, with various other forms of direct and indirect dissent or even mild insubordination being also brought into the equation. This name-calling was then deployed in an attempt to equate the African National Congress (ANC) with ETA, the IRA and the other forms of 'terrorism' about which Europe and America were becoming increasingly concerned. Neatly ignored in the analysis, as entirely irrelevant to the assessment of this 'terrorist threat', was the fact that South Africa was ruled by an undemocratic racist regime, which was not only terrorizing its Black majority but was also engaged in aggressive wars against, and the sponsoring of horrifically brutal insurgencies within, the states adjacent to its borders. Bizarrely inappropriate though the language of terrorism undoubtedly was, this ruse enjoyed a great success throughout the 1980s. As late as 1987, the US State Department included the ANC in its publication *Patterns of Global Terrorism*, and in October the same year the British Prime Minister characterized the group as a 'terrorist organization'. It came to an end only when the 'terrorism' finally became unnecessary, with the 'terrorist' movement's leader eventually being fêted by the United States President in Washington, a city which had itself been named after another violent subversive not dissimilar in stature.

It has been the United States that has been most prolific in its use of the jargon of terrorism in international relations, but it is that country which has also been loosest in its application of any coherent definition to the term. Distinctions between international, state-sponsored, transnational and purely domestic terrorism have come and gone as the US has sometimes condemned subversive violence and sometimes applauded it. At times, such as with the ANC and its neighbouring Namibian liberation movement SWAPO, it has seemed as though the US has been prepared to castigate as terrorist any challenge to any status quo, no matter how mild and popular the subversion or how dreadful or illegal the regime from which power has been sought to be wrested. On other occasions, however, the US has given the impression of being almost enthusiastically anarchic in its support for rebellious factions, most notably with UNITA in Angola, the Contras in Nicaragua and the anti-government forces in Soviet-backed Afghanistan in the 1980s. While occasional efforts have been made to distinguish international from other forms of 'terrorism', it has been neither a desire for linguistic clarity nor squeamishness about violence that has been the driving force behind US policy on terrorism. From the start of the Reagan presidency in 1981, the supposed problem of terrorism has been effectively harnessed as a branch of US foreign policy, with the condemnatory label being deployed to hurt the enemies of US interests while being withheld from US friends and client states, no matter how opprobrious their conduct might otherwise be.

Before the end of the Cold War, the great American enemy was of course the Soviet Union, and in the 1980s a plethora of books appeared dealing with Soviet involvement in terrorism. Replete with evocative titles such as *The Soviet Strategy of Terror*, these volumes sought to link the Soviets with the sort of indiscriminate killing for which the word terrorism stood in the public mind, and for which it was known there was universal disapproval. The then Director of the CIA, William Casey, contributed an essay along these lines called, 'The International Linkages – What Do We Know?' in a volume with the evocative title, *Hydra of Carnage*. At his first press conference as President Reagan's Secretary of State, Alexander Haig declared in his inimitable style that the Kremlin was today 'involved in conscious policies, in programs, if you will, which foster, support and expand this activity, which is haemorrhaging in many respects throughout the world today'. Connecting the Kremlin with terrorism suited the strategy of the first Reagan administration, since it helped to build up concern about the Soviets, which in turn made the greatly increased defence spending then envisaged by the White House more widely acceptable. The difficulty was that for decades the whole idea of terrorism had been limited to subversive groups acting in isolation. If the subject had up to that point enjoyed even a limited intellectual coherence, it had been rooted in the fact that state authorities were not capable of being terrorists. To solve this problem the US introduced the notion of 'state-sponsored terrorism', whereby it was rebellious groups which were acting in a subversive way in the traditional terrorist fashion, but which were doing so now under the protective aegis of a malevolent state, whose own forces were not however directly involved. Thus Soviet culpability lay not in any actions that its military forces might have been involved in, but rather in its provision of support for such 'terrorist groups' as the PLO and the ANC.

The absurdity of this manipulation of language became most fully apparent in the Middle East. The flimsy nature of the link between the PLO and the Soviets did not seem sufficient to underpin the international terrorist conspiracy for which it was the main evidence. This was particularly true when the connection was being most vividly emphasized, since by the early 1980s the mainstream PLO had long committed itself not to engage in political violence outside Israel and the Occupied Territories. One book, written by a distinguished academic expert and published at the height of the panic in 1982, opened with evidence for his argument that was revealingly comical in its emptiness:

Among the Palestine Liberation Organisation (PLO) and the Popular Front for the Liberation of Palestine (PFLP) rank-and-file in Southern Lebanon these days, the most prestigious badge of distinction that can be worn – weather permitting – is a Soviet-made fur hat. While not of the haute couture variety, Soviet fur hats are the latest thing in revolutionary chic, for possession of one in many parts of the world usually indicates that the owner is a graduate of one of the élite schools and camps operated by the USSR and its allies that train and indoctrinate terrorists and other revolutionaries. With each passing month, more and more fur hats appear in embattled Lebanon and, for that matter, in dozens of other locations around the world. Ironically, they may soon lose some of their prestige value as they become too commonplace.

In 1982, it was not international terrorism, or indeed any sort of terrorism, that had 'embattled Lebanon'. Ever since the 1967 war, Israel and its US ally had used the West's obsession with terrorism as a diplomatic weapon against the PLO, condemning as 'support for terrorism' any recognition that the movement managed to secure on the international front. When the organization secured the rights of a United Nations member nation in 1976, Israel's most senior delegate denounced the organization as a 'loose coalition of feuding terrorist gangs'. And when in 1977 the French authorities expelled from the country, rather than arrested, a senior PLO executive suspected of having been involved in the Munich Olympic killings, the Israeli government recalled its ambassador from Paris, expressing its concern that the incident amounted to 'abject surrender to the . . . threats of terror organizations'. International conferences were held at which the problem of terrorism was earnestly debated by Israeli and other Western 'experts'. One of the most prolific of these specialists was Benjamin Netanyahu, who was subsequently to become Prime Minister of Israel. In one of Netanyahu's edited volumes, *Terrorism: How the West Can Win*, the then Israeli ambassador to the United Nations described the 'war against terror' as 'part of a much larger struggle, one between the forces of civilisation and the forces of barbarism'. It was time, he declared, for the West to 'unite and fight to win the war against terrorism'.

It was this sort of language of counter-terrorism which the Israeli authorities also deployed by way of justification for their use of force both inside the territories they occupied and against neighbouring states. In 1978, a violent attack within Israel by the PLO's military wing, which involved twenty-five civilian casualties, sparked off a full-scale invasion of Lebanon in which some 2,000 people died and an estimated quarter of a million inhabitants were made homeless. Five years later, Lebanon was 'embattled' by a second Israeli invasion, this time far more ambitious in its plans and bloody in its execution. It has been estimated that some 18,000 people died in the course of 'Operation Peace in Galilee' and the siege of Beirut that followed it, the vast majority of them Palestinian and Lebanese civilians. Once again the alibi for this military offensive was a terrorist incident, on this occasion the attempted assassination of the Israeli ambassador to Britain in London, two days before the invasion was launched, an incident for which the PLO was not even responsible. In the distorted language of the times, none of this Israeli conduct was terrorism because it was not done by a subversive group or even by a sponsored subversive group but rather by the full military power of a heavily armed state. Once again, we have the double paradox that the greater the terror, and the more likely it is to have been committed by a Western nation or ally, the less the label of terrorism seems likely to be able to fit.

The military strength of the US and its ally in the Middle East means that neither has had to deploy clandestine, proxy groups to bring about its goals. These can usually be achieved by military operations executed with brutal transparency. For their opponents, however, engaging in such conventional warfare spells certain doom. This was the case in both the 1967 and 1973 wars, just as it was when the PLO tried to take on the full might of the Israeli army in the Occupied Territories for a brief period in 1968. For such groups it has not been obvious why the only method of warfare morally available should be one which necessitates their certain and speedy demise. The penalty for such inconvenient prudence has been to labour under the American-inspired banner of international terrorism. But it is better to have insults shouted at you in the shadows than to be shot dead quietly in the open.

The mobilization of the language of terrorism in aid of America's military efforts in the Middle East has been the final catastrophe for any remaining shred of integrity that the concept of terrorism might have retained after its imposed flirtation with the Soviet empire in the early 1980s and its earlier deployment to mask Israel's territorial ambitions. In the years since the 1982 invasion of the Lebanon, the subject's coherence has completely collapsed. The attacks on the French and US military presence in Beirut in October 1983 which claimed the lives of 300 men were immediately classed as acts of 'international terrorism', even though the carefully chosen targets were military in nature and the objective of the co-ordinated operation was not merely to communicate a message but to achieve through the strength of the force used a clear political end, the evacuation from the area of this multi-national force. The 'terrorist' label was not, however, appropriate to describe any of the subsequent aerial attacks on the Sheikh Abdullah barracks launched by the French air force, the revenge car bomb allegedly exploded by the CIA in the vicinity of a Hezbollah leader's office (which killed eighty) or the bombardment of the Lebanese coast by the battleship *New Jersey* which marked the American Marines' withdrawal from the area by raining shells as heavy as cars on to vulnerable villages along the coast. Always discriminating about the kind of death he condemns, the terrorist expert has no interest in any of these violent acts, just as such a person is uninterested in the fundamental question why the US Marines and the rest of the multinational force were in Beirut in the first place. But it is surely not irrelevant to a proper overall assessment of the situation which produced these 'terrorist' attacks on Western forces that the main goal of these armies – the reason they were in the Lebanon – was to return the country to Christian rule under the 1943 constitution, these Christians not only being probably in a minority but also being frequently indistinguishable from the Phalang-ists who had run riot in Sabra and Chatila in Beirut in 1982, reportedly killing over 2,000 defenceless civilians in just two days.

Nowhere is the subjugation of the terrorist label more obvious than in respect of the notion of the 'terrorist state', to which US policymakers increasingly turned during the 1980s. Having wrenched free of American domination in 1979, Iran was of course immediately placed on the list, not only because of Hezbollah's attacks on the Marines but also because of the hostage-taking to which every Westerner in Beirut had become exposed after the withdrawal of the multinational force. Israel has, however, never qualified for inclusion, not for its overt military terror of course but also not even for its involvement in the notorious Khiam prison, in which some 300 Lebanese Shias were held without charge or trial in unspeakable conditions of brutality by the Israeli-sponsored South Lebanon Army. Another annual entry in the American list has been Libya, whose various involvements in European subversive violence, though largely unproven, were what provided the justification for the attack on Tripoli and Benghazi by US warplanes ordered by President Reagan in 1986. The number of casualties which resulted from this non-terrorist piece of 'self-defence' – believed to be in the region of thirty-seven dead and ninety injured – marks Mr Reagan out as a more prolific killer of Libyans than General Gadaffi seems ever to have managed to be of Americans. Syria was thought to have been responsible for some of the attacks attributed to Libya, but this nation has drifted in and out of the list of terrorist states according to how well its wily ruler President Assad has been getting on with the Americans at any particular time. In a similar vein, Iraq had long been off the list despite the horrendous nature of the Saddam regime, until its (entirely orthodox and therefore 'non-terrorist') military invasion of Kuwait led to its sudden reinclusion in September 1990. The other regular entrants in this infamous list have all been as prominent for their anti-Americanism as for their 'terrorism' – North Korea, South Yemen and, again inevitably, the ubiquitously evil Cuba.

In view of the manipulation to which the terrorist label has been subject, it is not at all surprising that, by the 1990s, the phrase has lost all traces of what little linguistic discipline it might once have had. It now seems to describe any violence which appears political in nature and which is designed to hurt the West, such as the blowing up of the Pan Am jet over Lockerbie in 1988 and (though the facts are as yet unclear) the downing of a TWA jet off the US coast in 1996. It is now also the word that the media rush to when seeking pithily to explain an act of violence somewhere in the world for which no immediately materialistic (and therefore explicable) rationale presents itself. Thus the gassing of an underground transport system in Japan, the suicidal hijack of an Ethiopian jet off the African coast and the maverick postal violence of the American Unibomber are all classed as terrorist actions, rather than as the erratic, desperate criminality that each might in truth more accurately reflect. As Adrian Guelke has put it in the course of his recent brilliant study, *The Age of Terrorism and the International Political System*, 'Ironically, there would seem good reason to suppose that both the continuity and the coherence imposed on events by the concept of terrorism have been factors in the legitimization of political violence by removing from individuals joining underground organizations or even acting independently of any organization the psychological burden of justifying such violence *ab initio*.' Once the idea of terrorism insinuated itself into common usage in this way, it was only a matter of time before it came to be deployed to describe even non-violent conduct where what was sought to be communicated was a general moral disapproval. Thus in recent years we have had 'eco-terrorism', 'narco-terrorism' and even, after this or that health scare, 'consumer terrorism'. It is as though there is no mischief which does not need to be repackaged as a branch of terrorism for its full horror to be first savoured and then universally condemned.

All of this busy verbal inflation does not come from nowhere. The devastation wreaked on the meaning of terrorism in the 1980s left the word lying open on the ground, its inherent moral judgement exposed to all and available to be occupied by whatever freeloading moralist happened to be passing by. This linguistic anarchy is the price that has been paid for the calculated rape of meaning that had earlier occurred. Despite these consequences, the concept of terrorism remains fully on display in its true home, the Middle East, justifying Israeli assaults on Southern Lebanon in 1995 which involved violent attacks on a United Nations mission there and supposedly legitimizing Israeli demands for a continuing strong security presence in the Occupied Territories, despite commitments made internationally to the opposite effect. The idea of terrorism is not, however, an easily tamed one. That it can take on a destructive life of its own can be seen from the effect that it has had on the implementation of the Oslo Peace Accords, signed by the chairman of the PLO Yasser Arafat and the Prime Minister of Israel Yitzhak Rabin at a ceremony in the White House in 1994. Having secured the 'peace' for which it had long fought so aggressively, neither the US nor the Israeli leadership had any interest any longer in allowing this or that atrocity to destroy the process. The problem, however, was that atrocities were not merely atrocities, they were also 'acts of terrorism' to the 'defeat' of which all other policy objectives had for years been required to be subjugated. Having broken free of the language of terrorism to strike a deal with the arch 'terrorist' Yasser Arafat, both governments now found themselves hostage to the next atrocity, involuntarily beholden to the anxieties that they had earlier so successfully cultivated.

The result of this was that subversive violence which in itself could hardly be said to be capable of challenging the authority of the State of Israel in any meaningful sense was able disproportionately to influence the execution of the Accords. Its inevitable characterization as 'terrorism' fuelled public panic and led the previously terrorist-obsessed Israeli government to seem weak and inadequate. The Israeli right-wing opposition first articulated its opposition to Oslo and then secured political power through the language of terrorism. Arafat may have specifically repudiated the use of terrorist methods as long before Oslo as 1988, but as a result of the Accords the PLO had 'presided over a fantastic explosion of anti-Israeli terrorism', according to Benjamin Netanyahu, writing in 1995. From the hostile Arab perspective, the Accords were equally vulnerable to the sort of emotional havoc that a few well-timed bombs could cause. In late February and early March 1996, four suicide bombings in Israel caused heavy loss of life and helped create the conditions of paranoid insecurity which facilitated Netanyahu's rise to power. The United States President Bill Clinton, acting like an old-style Roman emperor in this new post-Cold War world, immediately summoned a 'Summit of Peacemakers' at Sharm El Sheikh in Egypt. The various world leaders who answered the American call agreed to 'promote co-ordination of efforts to stop acts of terror on bilateral, regional and international levels' and committed themselves to 'ensuring instigators of such acts are brought to justice; supporting efforts by all parties to prevent their territories from being used for terrorist purposes; and preventing terrorist organizations from engaging in recruitment, supplying arms; or fund raising'.

President Clinton knew that this was not just about

deploying the language of terrorism to buttress Israeli power in the normal way. The subject has also developed its own US domestic agenda. Every president since Reagan has felt duty-bound to frighten the American people with wild talk of the terrorist enemy within and without. One week after he had assumed office, Reagan had declared, 'Let terrorists beware that when the rules of international behaviour are violated, our policy will be one of swift and effective retribution.' George Bush had contributed a chapter to one of Netanyahu's alarmist collections in 1981, which was then reprinted in 1989 after Bush had become president. The front cover of another of Netanyahu's works, *Fighting Terrorism*, published in 1995, was emblazoned with the commendation 'excellent', offered by a still optimistic Robert Dole. Now Clinton stepped neatly into this new presidential tradition. As his close adviser Dick Morris later revealed, he had during 1996 advised the President of the three 'big things' that it would take for him to drag himself out of the third into the second tier of American leadership. The third of these was 'to break the international back of terrorism by economic and military action'. 'That's a good list,' Clinton had allegedly replied to the adviser. 'It puts things into perspective.'

Chapter 4
The True Threat from Terrorism

The concept of terrorism is more than merely the meaning-less plaything of international diplomacy. In recent years it has also been deployed within democratic states so as drastically to restructure the relationship between the individual and the state, to the former's profound disad-vantage. This is the meaning of the fourth of the heretical propositions set out at the start of this essay, that while democracy may indeed be threatened in our artificial 'age of terrorism', the danger to its integrity comes more from the terrorists' opponents, the states and their armed and police forces, than from the so-called terrorists themselves. Viewed in historical perspective, it is remarkable how fear of terrorism has justified legal changes that would other-wise surely have been unthinkable.

Take as our first instance the United States of America. It will come as no surprise that there are at least four definitions of terrorism lurking within the law, with each being sprung into action by the authorities as and when it is required. In the absence of much serious subversive violence within its borders, the US has dealt over many years with its indigenous 'terrorism' not as a universal threat requiring special measures but as a series of particu-lar forms of criminality, which is all generally that these groups have ever amounted to. After the Oklahoma bomb-ing in April 1995, however, the atmosphere quickly changed, with the Clinton administration proposing that the FBI be given access to personal financial records, including bank accounts and credit card and telephone bills, to assist their investigations, and also that the Bureau be given new wiretapping powers. Inevitably there has also been a foreign dimension. Speedy procedures to deport aliens who are 'suspected terrorists' have also been sought. In the mammoth Terrorism Prevention Act 1996 that followed Clinton's politically contrived concentration on the 'terrorist threat', not even the constitutionally protected right to free speech escaped attention. Congress has gone out of its way, under the guise of counter-terrorism, to starve foreign groups inimical to government interests of the capacity to communicate directly to the American people. The Act allows the Secretary of State to designate a group a foreign terrorist organization, after which it becomes a criminal offence to provide material for it. Following on such a designation, the authorities may order the freezing of the group's financial assets. Free speech remains, but no one will be listening. In a separate and particularly draconian section, the Act makes it an offence for a US citizen to engage in various financial transactions with countries deemed by the administration to be 'terrorist states'. We saw earlier how this label has degenerated into little more than a contrivance of US foreign policy. Now we see it being deployed to consolidate US power over the whole world, since in the post-Cold War era any state refusing to acquiesce to US interests risks a designation that will deprive it not only of American business, but of all business everywhere in which Americans are involved, which in practical terms means most of the business in the developed world.

This latter section has provoked an angry response from the European Union, but here too there has been a transformation in the nature of policing, almost all of it covertly effected and much of it driven by a perception that the 'war against terrorism' requires a common police front-line. In 1976, an informal liaison group to deal with terrorism, policing and customs issues of common interest was set up on a purely informal basis within the European Community. Named TREVI, this body provided an inter-governmental forum with meetings every six months at ministerial and official level. TREVI was joined in 1979 by the EU-wide Police Working Group on Terrorism (PWGOT), made up of representatives of all the then EC countries plus Finland, Norway and Sweden. In 1990, TREVI secured a permanent secretariat and in the years that followed this initiative the practice grew of exchanging 'counter-terrorism liaison officers' between states in the Union, whose role it was (and remains) to provide the host police forces with information and advice on terrorism. None of these developments has been subject to any statutory or political control, a state of affairs that is likely to persist even after the EU Council of Justice and Home Affairs, set up under the Maastricht Treaty in 1992, has been fully implemented. The complaint is of course not about the principle of co-operation in the proper discharge of police duties in respect of law enforcement; it is about the way in which such an informal network has been allowed to develop on the margins of legality and without adequately transparent political accountability. Terrorism may not have been the sole driving force behind these developments, but the secrecy and autonomy in which these police operations are perpetually shrouded owes much to the intimidatory power of the label.

It is to the United Kingdom that pessimists about our freedom should look for a depressing glimpse of the future. Britain has been exposed more than most nations to the 'counter-terrorism' ethos on account of a combination of three factors: a genuine problem of violent subversion in Northern Ireland; a government unsympathetic to civil liberties which enjoyed a continuous hold on power for eighteen years; and the absence of many of the checks and balances on executive power that are to be found in most Western democratic nations. The effect of the supposed necessities of terrorism on the civil liberties of the citizen has been quite extraordinary. In Northern Ireland, the authorities first reacted to subversive violence with conduct that was at and beyond the margins of illegality. The internment of suspected members of the IRA was introduced in 1971 and held sway as a principal policy for some four years, during which allegations of torture and ill-treatment were frequently made in respect of the treatment of many of those who were then in police custody. This phase of the conflict was also marked by the highest levels of deaths that have been endured in the Province since the disorder began, a worrying proportion of which at this time were at the hands of the security forces. The most controversial of such incidents was the shooting dead of fourteen unarmed protesters in Derry on 30 January 1972, in an incident which was subsequently to enter Irish nationalist folklore as 'Bloody Sunday'.

From about the mid-1970s, the state embarked on a new tactic of criminalization, whereby subversive violence was no longer to be dealt with by military-style means but was rather to be processed through the courts as a brand of terrorist criminality. The propaganda advantages to the authorities from this change of tack were obvious, but the unattractive reality continued to be that the subversives enjoyed a large measure of active and passive support within their own communities and this was not likely to be easily changed by a state-sponsored labelling exercise. The policy of criminalization and of 'police primacy' therefore inevitably required the wholesale truncation of the rule of law if it was to be effective. This is exactly what has happened in Northern Ireland when the new approach began to take effect in the mid-1970s. The breadth of the criminal law was immeasurably widened so as to facilitate the bringing of charges against suspected 'terrorists'. Those who are arrested may be denied access to a lawyer for up to forty-eight hours and may be held in custody without charge for as long as seven days. The right to silence, both for a suspect in a police cell and an accused before a court, has been emasculated and may now only very rarely be effectively invoked. Trial by jury has become a thing of the past for 'terrorist' crimes, with all such cases now being heard by a judge sitting alone. Despite the absence of political violence in Northern Ireland, the government has not rushed to the resuscitate the rule of law.

These modifications to the rule of law have been particular to Northern Ireland, but the changes that have occurred in the rest of the United Kingdom on the basis of the supposed threat of terrorism have in many ways been far more sinister and have also survived the outbreak of peace. To start with, the driving force behind the restriction of civil liberties was the violence in Northern Ireland. Thus, in legislation passed in 1974, Parliament empowered the authorities to proscribe 'terrorist' organizations and to arrest without warrant persons suspected of being involved in 'terrorism', if needs be restricting their movement within the UK through the use of a form of internal banishment called 'exclusion orders'. These powers were initially deployed only against persons suspected of involvement in Northern Ireland-related violence, which was an important qualification given that the Act defined terrorism in the broadest possible terms as 'the use of violence for political ends', including 'any use of violence for the purpose of putting the public or any section of the public in fear'. It was therefore an important but barely noticed moment when in 1984, in the midst of the scare about international terrorism that marked the first Reagan presidency, Parliament agreed to extend the arrest and detention powers in the terrorism legislation to suspected 'international terrorists'. It has been on the basis of the need to deal with 'international' as well as Northern Ireland-related 'terrorism' that the police have subsequently secured for themselves unprecedently wide powers to stop and search vehicles and pedestrians and to throw up cordons around whole areas as part of this or that counter-terrorism operation.

The way in which these latter powers were secured is characteristic of how the fear of terrorism is deployed by the authorities to coerce the democratic process into compliance with its will. On Friday, 29 March 1996, it emerged that in the government's view there was an urgent need for fresh counter-terrorism law, so as to prevent an imminent IRA campaign which it was said was set to commence in Britain in the course of the next few days, to commemorate the eightieth anniversary of the Easter Rising. The official opposition was quickly tamed by a couple of confidential briefings and the Bill was printed, and rushed through both the House of Commons and the House of Lords in the course of no more than a couple of days in the following week, which was Easter week. A measure that had never been publicly heard of on a Friday was law by the following Wednesday. Those few MPs who expressed concern about this process in the Commons found that the government and opposition were not only prepared to agree the Bill but were also agreed about pushing it through with no more than a few hours of debate permitted to discuss its merits. No IRA campaign subsequently occurred, despite the fact that the new powers did not appear to have been deployed immediately or extensively by the police. Critics of the measure pointed out that it could hardly have come as such a sudden surprise to the police and Security Service that the eightieth anniversary of Easter Week was due in 1996. It also did not seem to have occurred to the planners of the Bill that the commemoration of Easter 1916 was in any event not due in the week that the legislation was enacted, since Easter is a movable feast and Easter in 1916 had occurred in late rather than early April.

None of this mattered to Parliament, which allowed the spell waved by the repressive wand of 'counter-terrorism' to magic away freedoms which had been hard won over generations of civil libertarian struggle. The same rhetorical power may well shortly ensure the application of the 'terrorism' laws to domestic subversives, such as the environmental and animal rights groups, that have engaged so actively and successfully in direct action in recent years. In late 1996, it almost secured a place on the statute books for a Private Member's Bill which would have criminalized in Britain the planning of 'terrorist' crimes abroad. Given the broad way in which terrorism is defined in British law, condemning all violence for political ends, this was a truly outrageous proposal, which risked turning the British authorities into the law-enforcement agencies of various police states. The authoritarian leaders of China, Burma and Indonesia, for example, would no doubt have welcomed the opportunity to have had those of their courageous opponents who have escaped to Britain transformed into convicted terrorists for the crime of continuing to try to stand up to them. The proposal has never fully disappeared from the political agenda. The ultimate degradation of language will have been reached when it will have become possible to brand the Dalai Lama as an international terrorist for his defiance of China's will in Tibet.

Chapter 5
Looking Ahead

The central argument in this essay has a simplicity that is almost naive. There is a depressingly large amount of political violence in the world and many ways in which it manifests itself. These include war, civil war, covert war conducted by proxies, guerrilla warfare, large-scale communal fighting and the sort of isolated subversive violence that has come to be known as terrorism. Each of these ways of engaging in conflict may involve but does not necessitate the use of terror as a political weapon. By terror, we mean the launching of a reckless or consciously indiscriminate attack on civilians in order to communicate a political message to a third party, who will invariably be the real enemy. Viewed in this way, terror can be seen for what it is, a tactic available to any combatant or covert combatant in any hostile situation. We have recounted examples of terror being used in the Second World War, by both Churchill and Truman as well as by Hitler. We have also seen how the tactic was deployed in the course of various colonial conflicts in Africa in the 1950s and 1960s. It is a sadly familiar feature of the part-communal, part-separatist violence that has engulfed Sri Lanka and the Punjabi region of India from the early 1980s. Terror is of course also one of the tactics to which many subversive groups – 'terrorists' in the sense just described – have turned when they have been engaged in a covert campaign of sporadic violence against their own national authorities. Indeed because of the relative ineffectiveness of this kind of violence when targeted solely on well-defended official and military targets, we have seen how engagement in it, however focused initially, seems to lead almost inevitably to more and more killing of civilians.

Three points emerge from viewing 'terror' and 'terrorism' separately in the way described above. First, terror is not all that those we describe as terrorists do. Indeed it is something which they might never do or might strive always to avoid. Second, 'terrorists' have no monopoly on terror. It is a tactic available to all, and has frequently been employed with deadly abandon in non-terrorist conflict situations. Third, the immorality of engaging in violent conflict for political ends can never be simply assumed, and this is as true of terrorist campaigns as it is of any other form of political warfare. Our society has been built on bloodshed and has defended itself violently when the need has arisen. Political violence has made us what we are. It is not even clear that the tactic of political terror is always necessarily wrong in every conflict situation. Terrible examples of just this form of warfare during the Second World War are still felt by many to have been a horrible necessity. What we can be slightly more sure about is that the use of the tactic of terror by a terrorist group will invariably be ill advised, at least for reasons of inefficacy if not also for reasons of immorality. But it is quite impossible to say *a priori* that the use of violence short of terror by any subversive group is necessarily wrong. Everything depends on context. What is heroic under an authoritarian regime will be less so in a properly functioning democracy. The violent defenders of a community oppressed by the brutality of a police-state are in a different category from young men and women whose violence is proactive and unprovoked by earlier, direct aggression. The choices forced on a contemporary Nelson Mandela cannot be equated with those of a latter-day Andreas Baader.

The language of terrorism in its modern usage cuts across all these distinctions. It rushes to condemn wherever it finds political violence of which it disapproves. By eliding terror and terrorism, it wrongly suggests that only the terrorist engages in terror. It ignores not only political context but also our history, and that commitment to justice and fairness which has made us less uncivilized than we might otherwise have been. It is a verbal Trojan horse through which much of the liberty and freedom that make us what we are risks being set aside by the repressive reflexes of the 'counter-terrorist' state. The stakes here are higher than are usually supposed. It has only been in the twentieth century that the moral force of democracy has finally triumphed against the rival opposition of fascism and of communism. The form of this victory is still up for grabs. The optimist will say that Western society is bound to continue to develop along truly democratic lines, slowly but inexorably growing into a culture in which civil liberties and human dignity are universally respected and in which our political leaders are routinely not only elected but also held genuinely accountable for the power that they exercise. This benign scenario is however by no means inevitable. The victory that the democratic West has won over its fascist and communist opponents was only possible after the people of the West had won democracy for themselves, against ruling élites that were on the whole markedly disinclined to surrender their privilege. It is this internal battle that has been only half-won.

The West remains a place of great inequality and injustice, despite its apparent commitment to popular rule. The winning of the franchise has not yet produced the equality of opportunity and the universal respect for human dignity which many of its supporters assumed would be its inevitable consequence. Democracy in the West needs to be revived and reinvigorated so that its early promise can finally be realised. Those who have most to lose from a change of this sort have never truly conceded victory to the democratic revolutionaries. They are always vigilant for the chance to turn back the egalitarian tide. If they are successful, we will have a different more malign form of democracy in the future, one in which the form of self-government may remain ostentatiously in place but in which real power will be exercised elsewhere, without publicity, accountability or vulnerability to popular pressure. In such a society, it will be vital to extinguish all manifestations of public discontent. The self-justifying authoritarianism of the exigencies of 'counter-terrorism' will then achieve its full flowering, as the chief means of quietly, apparently morally, destroying all unacceptable dissent. It is for the reader to evaluate which scenario is the more likely to result. We can only be sure of one thing, at the end of this inquiry. The loose language of terrorism has become too dangerous to be acceptable in any healthy democracy.

Further Reading

It will come as no surprise to readers who have got this far that few of the specialist academic works on terrorism, of which there are hundreds, share the perspective that has been developed in this essay. Typical of the mainstream genre from whose title one of our central themes is drawn is Walter Laqueur's influential *The Age of Terrorism* (Boston and London, 1987). A good academic treatment of the subject is Grant Wardlaw, *Political Terrorism: Theory, Tactics, and Counter-Measures* (Cambridge, 2nd edn, 1989). The careful scholar alluded to on p. 17 above is A. P. Schmid, whose book (with A. J. Longman), *Political Terrorism: A New Guide to Actors, Authors, Concepts, Data Bases, Theories and Literature* (Amsterdam, 1988) is a significant contribution to the literature. By far the best recent study of the subject of terrorism as a whole is Adrian Guelke, *The Age of Terrorism and the International Political System* (London and New York, 1995), whose influence I am delighted to aknowledge. Another major influence has been Noam Chomsky, whose political writings as a whole resound with a sceptical integrity which I have tried here to imitate if not emulate. On terrorism in particular see his *The Culture of Terrorism* (Boston, 1988). Some of the best work on terrorism does not describe itself as such, preferring to deal with the real issue of the morality of engaging in subversive violence. See in particular David Miller, 'The Use and Abuse of Political Violence', *Political Studies*, 32 (1984), pp. 401–19, and Tony Honoré, 'The Right to Rebel',

Oxford Journal of Legal Studies, 8 (1988), pp. 34–54. Both essays are reprinted in C. A. Gearty (ed.), *Terrorism* (Aldershot, 1996), in the introduction to which volume I develop some of the themes discussed here. For an earlier version of the central argument in this essay, developed at somewhat greater length but (I think now) less completely, see my *Terror* (London, 1991).

The books mentioned in the text are, in alphabetical order, S. T. Francis, *The Soviet Strategy of Terror* (Washington DC, 1981); Adrian Guelke, *The Age of Terrorism and the International Political System* (London and New York, 1995); Josephus, *The Jewish War* (Harmondsworth, 1970); N. C. Livingstone, *The War against Terrorism* (Lexington, 1982); Dick Morris, *Behind the Oval Office* (New York, 1996); Benjamin Netanyahu, *Fighting Terrorism* (London, 1996); Benjamin Netanyahu (ed.), *International Terrorism: Challenge and Response* (New Brunswick, N. J., 1989); Benjamin Netanyahu (ed.), *Terrorism: How the West Can Win* (London, 1986); and U. Ra'anan, R. L. Pfaltzgraff, R. H. Shultz, E. Halperin and I. Lukes, *Hydra of Carnage* (Lexington, 1986).